THE RELIGION
THAT WAS CHANGED
BY ITS OWN
PRIESTHOOD

THE RELIGION
THAT WAS CHANGED
BY ITS OWN
PRIESTHOOD

LENNART WINGARDH

ARPress
ILLUMINATING IDEAS.
EMPOWERING VOICES

ARPress
45 Dan Road Suite 5
Canton, MA 02021

Hotline: 1(888) 821-0229
Fax: 1(508) 545-7580

Ordering Information:
Quantity sales. Special discounts are available on quantity purchases by corporations, associations, and others. For details, contact the publisher at the address above.

Printed in the United States of America.

ISBN-13:   Softcover   979-8-89330-274-5
            eBook   979-8-89330-273-8

Library of Congress Control Number: 2024901490

TABLE OF CONTENTS

D ear Reader, it is of the utmost importance that you learn that the original religion - that the only living God gave to Jesus to spread out, was the same monotheistic (one-God) religion that HE had given to the Prophet Moses for His Jewish people.

You need to understand that this religion of God was changed by its own priesthood to the current man-made trinity religion, that's known as Christianity.

You must also understand and accept that anything that God put's in place that's changed by a human being, becomes corrupted and unusable from the point of view of God – making it a sin of major consequence.

In the Qur'an God says that HE has no son, which is a clear indication that HE isn't in agreement with the (man-made) Nicene Creed that states that Jesus is His son, which HE refutes, again and again! All those implicated become sinners. And, all sinners have but one destiny – Hell! Depending on the kind of sin, the sinner will suffer the rest of Eternity in any of levels one to seven, suffering the most in the seventh level.

Very unfortunately, all who worship Jesus, a Prophet of God, instead of worshipping the Only Living God, have that same destiny - Hell!

The Lord wants to be worshiped *"with the Heart".* In Isaiah 29:13, *we learn that HE said, "These people claim to worship me, but their words are meaningless and their hearts are somewhere else. Their religion is nothing but human rules and traditions."*

L ennart possesses in-depth knowledge of the two Abrahamic Scriptures, the Jewish Bible and the Qur'an of Islam, in addition to the Christian Bible, which comprises three books, the Jewish Bible that became named The Old Testament, the New Testament and the Book of Revelation that have no interrelation. The new Roman trinity Christians simply '*brought them together*' to make the Christian Bible.

Author of the book, **'*The Unfortunate Destiny of Our Planet*'**
that provides a powerful linkage to this book, putting in
your hands a vastness of knowledge.

PREFACE

This book deals with how God's original Monotheistic (one God) religion that HE gave to Jesus to be spread in Israel as well as in other countries. It was replaced by its Christian priesthood, who put in its place a totally different trinity (pagan) cult, similar to the pagan ones in existence, example the Egyptian Isis trinity cult

Although not seeming to be of mayor consequence, it was, as we can understand, unacceptable to the Only Living God, since any change and especially to His unique Monotheistic religion, mainly, the creation of an inexistent son of His – who, it was mandated, must be worshipped instead of Him.

I state that still at this time 'Nobody' has understood - to any degree - the severity of what was done at the bishops unique conference, 'under the auspices of Roman pagan Caesar Constantine I, (the Great) in Nicaea, Turkey.

It would, however, come to cause changes of calamitous proportion of all the kinds that I believe wouldn't have taken place within the realms of God's Monotheistic (one god) religion, such as (examples):

The alteration of the gospels, falsifying them to make them to fit into the new false Christian trinity religion and bible, used in many applications, the one most used being, I believe to swear the truth – under oath.

In November 1095, Pope Urban II delivered a famous sermon at the Council of Clermont in which he called for Christians to unite and recapture the city of Jerusalem from Muslims, inciting the First Crusade. Just imagine, the leader of the falsest religion (not of God) – Christianity - pushing it to go out and make war against the religion – Islam - that the One and Only God put in place. It was, I believe the war(s) that involved the greatest amount of people.

The 'Spanish Inquisition - a powerful office set up within the Catholic (trinity) Church to root out and punish(what was believed to be heresy) throughout Europe and the Americas. Beginning in the 12th century and continuing for hundreds of years, the Inquisition is infamous for the cruelty of its tortures and its persecution of Jews and Muslims – the only two Abrahamic religions of the Only Living God. Columbus, who was given criminals, murderers and other, such as undesired priests who Spain was happy to get rid of (poor Latin America) to fill his three ships with destination to the unknown - to Latin America and the Caribbean.

I believe it was one of the most atrocious and brutal conquests committed by any country involving the Catholic Church – with the falsest religion of all times being taught - to the many different Indigenous populations. A great amount of its populations died from illnesses the Spaniards brought with them unknown to the 'locals', including syphilis and gonorrhea against which they weren't prepared, in addition to all the atrocious onslaughts using for that time extraordinarily powerful weapons for mass-extinction never seen before in that extensive region.

I lived in several countries, Cuba, Mexico, Colombia and Venezuela and traveled there very extensively and had the opportunity to see the consequences of what the church had done, mandating I say, total submission from the poor peoples to the Catholic Church, influencing their ways of thinking and living, and cultures. While the church destroyed their mentalities by teaching a false religion and worshipping an inexistent son of God, the military in principle enslaved the people and demanded the people to give them their possessions and sent everything of value either to their majesties of Spain or to be kept in the vaults of the Vatican, the Indians becoming poorer and poorer. Latin America, the Southern part of the Western Hemisphere, extensively as the result of the kinds of (bad) people who arrived there, the Spanish militaries and priests, beginning in the year 1494, is the poorest and most underdeveloped of all regions of our planet.

I say that this gives an idea of the enormous successes of Satan, our wicked enemy and Nemesis has been in taking away mankind from the way of God, by standing in his/her/our way as he promised to God, as God describes it in the Qur'an that you'll find in my book, 'The Unfortunate Destiny of our Planet'.

INTRODUCTION

Dear Reader, one of the foremost purposes of this book, is to provide to you clearcut evidence, that Christianity isn't the religion that Almighty God gave to Jesus, because it was changed along the way corrupting it extensively.

Before continuing, I want to again mention my recently published Book titled, '*The Unfortunate Destiny of our planet*'. Although it doesn't directly deal with religion, it brings into the picture matters from the Jewish Torah, parts of which were used in the formulation of the Christian trinity religion. At issue (very important) is that some of the texts that were taken from the TORAH had been changed, something that deeply affected the formulation of the man-made Nicene Creed of the trinity Christianity.

It's vitally important to know that all religions, excepting the two that God created, the Jewish and Islam, have nothing to do with God. You will learn that they were originated, one way or the other, by the evil doings of Satan who induced his ideas of deceit into the minds of human beings. But even God's two religions were strongly affected by Satan, taking its people away from God, as Satan told God he would do. We shall return to this matter.

Many people don't (want to) believe that God exists. HE is our uncontested Creator, Master, Ruler and Owner of everything, who demands that we worship only Him - the only living God, in our hearts (with feeling), and not with empty words - and obey His Commandments. The same ones that HE had previously given to Moses for the Jewish people, are valid for all mankind.

God, the almighty Creator has inimitable powers, which are beyond our capabilities to understand. HE can see what we call the future, as well as the past and can create anything at His will. I mention this because of things that happened to and around Jesus that can't be explained with human logic.

At the other end of the spectrum, is Satan, the evil-doer, the self-proclaimed enemy of mankind who works 24/7 to make man – you, me and everybody - to sin, thereby falling away from God. Satan lives on a different dimension, unseen to mankind, while he sees us.

Sadly, very few people seem to believe that Satan exists or don't care, which is to the detriment of those who God calls unbelievers. You need to know that God allows man – you and everybody - to do whatever we desire; through '*the free will*' HE gave us.

Satan knows of our free will and takes advantage of it to shatter our lives. He is attentive to the doings of every individual, looking at ways to make him/her to fall in his traps of deceit. In most cases unfortunately, it takes the sinner to perdition with eternal atrocious suffering in Hell.

The best way for Satan to cause man to fall away from God is by affecting the fate. This is so, because when human beings worship anything or anybody who isn't the only living God, including Jesus, the virgin Mary and all man-made saints, they are no longer, who God calls believers.

Of all religions, only the Jewish and the Prophet Mohammad's original Sunni religion of Islam originated from God. You ask, what about the Christian trinity religion? The answer is that the religion that God gave to His Prophet Jesus to spread, was Monotheistic (one God), the same HE had given to Moses lasted short of three-hundred years, when it was changed, as we shall learn how.

The result of this is ruinous for most people - as God reveals in the Qur'an, chapter 38:84-85 - wherein HE says HE will fill Hell with all who follow Satan, who HE calls unbelievers.

I realize that to most people this must sound unreal. But, if you had taken time, to study the End-of-Time prophecies of God, I guarantee you would know and think differently.

In the Book of the prophet Isaiah (in the Good News Bible, chapter 43:10 that I suggest you read, God declares that *HE is the only God that exists and that besides Him there is no other God*. HE sees and knows everything everywhere, why nothing is unknown or hidden from Him, as HE reveals in the Book of Jeremiah 23:23 in the Jewish Bible.

Through His Prophet Moses, God instituted the TORAH - that HE called *His LAW* that's the introduction to the Jewish Bible. But, in accordance to what God told His Prophet Jeremiah 8:8, *His LAW (*the TORAH*) had been changed (*corrupted*)*, so, it was no longer valid.

There's only one explanation to how this could happen and that was Satan whispering his ideas of deceit into the Jewish Rabbis in charge of the Bible.

In Qur'an 5:46, God reveals that HE gave Jesus the (Jewish) Torah with light and guidance, that HE previously had given to His prophet Moses. God goes on saying that HE also gave Jesus, the son of Mary, the Gospels, (as they were going to be written by the Apostols of Jesus) with light and guidance. But, the original Gospels, as God gave them to Jesus later-on were re-written by the Catholic Church to fit their new Christian trinity religion. In doing so, we realize that the Monotheistic (one god only) religion that God had given to Jesus, became corrupted, false in all senses, no longer valid.

Jesus walked with his Disciples to distant locations to introduce the Monotheistic religion that God had given to him to spread, which in time became known as Christianity.

As we know, the work of Jesus to bring out God's Monotheistic religion was cut short by Caiaphas the Jewish High priest in Jerusalem in the year 33 AD. That was when Caiaphas and His priests went after Jesus, trying to kill him to get him out of the way. Caiaphas did it because he was afraid of the teachings of Jesus that had begun to cause commotion amongst the Jews.

But, in Qur'an 4:157-158, God reveals that Jesus was neither killed nor crucified, and also that HE took Jesus up to heaven, obviously to avoid that he be badly treated. But there was another reason as well, why God took away (disappeared) Jesus.

The question is, if it wasn't Jesus that was crucified and died, who was it then who died on the cross, who to this day is being worshipped as the (inexistent) son of God, a god? We shall return to these critically important matters.

With Jesus out of the way after three years, the Monotheistic religion that God had given to spread out, went on without a leader. It's obvious that the absence of active leadership - over time - would affect the faith of the Christian church leaders. How, you ask, could anything affect this religion?

It happened as the result of the great distances between the Churches at the time, that led to having minimal contact between them, if any.

As time passed, and as the result of the lack of ongoing contact, because who was there to make sure God's unique (Monotheistic) religion that HE had given to Jesus, was kept on course among the Church leaders? Be sure that their beliefs went fading at the same time that they became affected by the pagan beliefs of the people amongst whom they worked. It is so, especially because the early generations of new Christians, converted from mainly prevailing pagan trinity cults, why it was part of their upbringing. There isn't the least doubt that the Egyptian pagan Isis trinity cult that had been adopted by the Roman empire, sometime before, had a strong effect upon them.

This is where Satan, the unseen deceiver came into the picture, of which God repeatedly warns about in the Qur'an, when He says "*Children of Adam be careful so that Satan doesn't deceive you*".

We need to know that pagan religions were the doings of Satan, who induces his ideas of what he wants us to believe into the minds of people, who are in search of God. Thus, Satan misleads them (us) away from God exactly as God reveals in the Qur'an that Satan promised to Him, he would do, sometime after His creation of Adam. We shall return to this important matter.

Satan has shown he is immensely clever, since he has managed to make himself to appear as inexistant, which is why nobody ever mentions him, something that obviously is to the detriment of those who follow him; believe it or not, the great majority of us.

What's so awful, is that this invisible sinister being, our Nemesis, may be right besides those of us who he has found are easy to make to fall *in his traps of deceit*, and we don't have the faintest idea that he is there, inducing ideas into our minds that are as our own, and, worst of all, to our liking. But, categorically not to the liking of God.

Before continuing I want to tell you about something that happened to me when I was six years of age.

I am Swedish, but was born in Cuba on July 19, 1934, in a Dairy Farm a few miles away from a small city by the name of Bayamo, a very historical city. I began early on to attend a Catholic school that was part of a convent (monastery) operated by nuns. My parents (father Swedish and mother German) placed me there in pre-kinder, from the age of five, despite that they weren't Catholic, because it was the best school around.

 You wonder why this is important. It is, because the religious teaching imparted in Catholic schools was (is) to worship mainly Jesus instead of God; and we were taught to pray to Jesus every evening when going to bed, which I did.

But and this is what happened to me one evening, in my sixth year, when I was praying. A voice suddenly talked to me loud and clear saying, *"Lennart, don't worship Jesus, worship God."* That was it. I remember it as if it was yesterday. It didn't change what I was being taught in school that Jesus was the son of God. But, from that moment on I prayed only to God, as I still do.

The question I pose is why this happened to me? At the time the incident took place I was too young to pay attention to it. But about forty plus years later, it came back to me.

It's just over forty years ago, when I became interested in the Ancient Prophecies of God that are related to *the End of the World* (of our planet). I dedicated lots of time to make extensive studies, spending thousands of hours to learn everything I could about this matter. It culminated in the book that was printed by mid-two-thousand and twenty-three titled, The Unfortunate Destiny of Our Planet.

I was doing my research when I began to find occurrences that directly and indirectly were related to Christianity, something that made me remember the voice that talked to me.

There must have been a reason that the voice talked to me. Because of that unique experience as a little boy, I took time to check out the Christian Bible, comparing it to what God says about Jesus in the Qur'an and there is a lot.

Because of what I learned; I decided to write this Book. There are quite a few things that take place in my book *The Unfortunate Destiny of Our Planet* that go back all the way to God's creation of Adam, which impacted the formation of the Christian trinity religion, put in place by the Christian priesthood, who I believe, knew practically nothing about God. Later on, in our time, Christianity began to split, into thousands of churches, the main objective of them for its founders was (is) to make money to fill their pockets, as God reveals in the Qur'an – something that HE is against. This is so, because an extensive part of the money from the collections is used to enrich themselves instead of being used for matters of the church including charities.

In the New Testament it's written that Jesus was tempted by Satan, which is the only thing that's said about Satan. I have my doubts that what's written really happened, for the reason(s) that I shall mention as we go. I'll bring in much more about Satan, who, according to God, came to be shortly after His creation of Adam, as God describes it in the Qur'an.

Herein, you'll learn who Satan is, and how he is, full speed, in the process of taking mankind – most of us – away from God, about which God said that HE would make sure that all who were following Satan would go with him to Hell and be with him for all eternity.

As I read the New Testament over and over, to learn about Jesus, which I hadn't done before in such detail, I made a discomforting discovery; it was that God, or rather His voice, isn't heard anywhere, not even once therein.

The Jewish Bible was originated by God, wherein HE talks to His Prophets. Later on, HE authored the Qur'an, which means that God was the only voice that was (is) heard, even if many times HE makes it sound as if it's His Prophet Muhammad who talks.

It was strange, I thought, when I compared it to the Jewish Bible, wherein God talked to His Jewish People through many Prophets, His Messengers, who He occasionally also called His Warners (Warners of future disasters).

I learned that the author of the Qur'an was God himself, who transferred the texts orally by His archangel Gabriel to the Prophet Mohammad, whom Gabriel met with in excess of twenty-thousand times, as was recorded.

Jesus isn't mentioned, more than indirectly, (as a future Prophet) by God through the Prophet Moses in the Jewish Bible;

God, called Allah in Arabic, mentions Jesus many times in the Qur'an. Chapters 19, titled Miriam or Mary, and in extensive parts of Chapter 3 named after the father of Mary, A'lay Imran, dedicated to Jesus and His mother, the then virgin Mary.

When I first read the Qur'an, I learned that God never refers to Jesus, as His son, which I thought was strange since Christians believe he is the son of God. On the contrary, in the Qur'an God refutes the belief that HE has a son, and HE is the One who knows the best.

HE has said that those who believe HE has a son and worship him are sinners and unbelievers (of Him).

Learning about Jesus, who he was, and very importantly what and who He was not, is important for many reasons. In reading the Qur'an I found that mostly everything about Jesus differs from what's written in the New Testament and in the Book of Revelation.

Circumstances related to the birth and to the virgin Mary differ completely in the New Testament. Very strange. How could it be?

The Christian New Testament was written by the Roman Catholic priesthood some time beginning after the Bishops Conference at Nicaea, Turkey in the year 325AD. That was when the Christian Trinity Creed or Dogma known as *'The Nicene Creed'* was instituted. The New Testament is composed of four Gospels with the names of four Apostles and a series of books of his Disciples.

In the Christian Bible was added *The Book of Revelation* that is unrelated to the New Testament, why it has nothing doing there.

This PowerPoint Chart was developed by me to give an idea of '*Occurrences*' that took mainly place between Adam & Eve and Satan, and, of the change of Gods Monotheistic religion, as revealed by God that's vitally important to know. The Roman Catholic church based its Trinity religion (cult) on texts from the Jewish Torah which them unknowing had been changed.

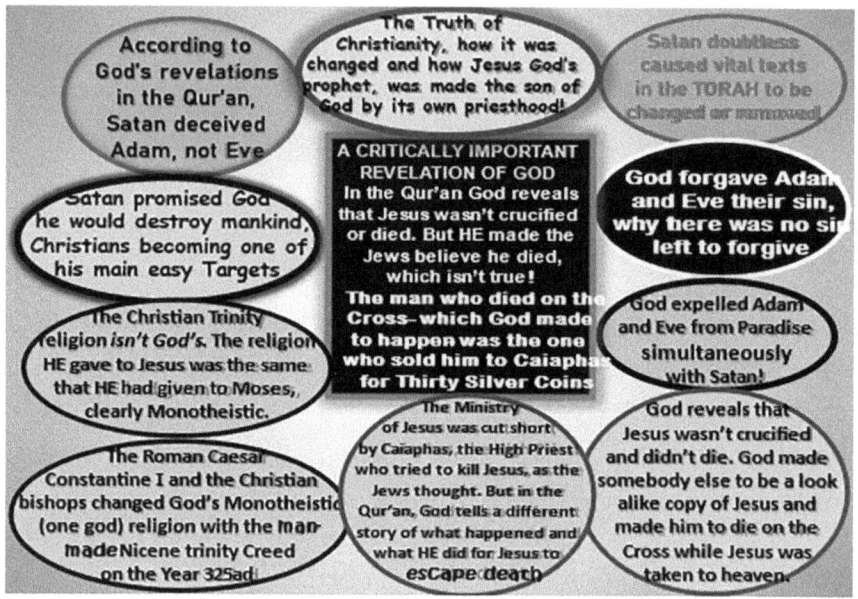

The most significant 'event' is described in the black oval with white text to the right that says that '*God forgave Adam & Eve their sin*', which means there wasn't any sin left to be forgiven by God, which goes against what's said in the Torah.

Another just as important 'event' is written in the Centre board relative to the death of Jesus. What God reveals in the Qur'an, is different to what's written in the New Testament and is doubtless the true version, because what God says is always right.

These are the two most significant events that contradict what Christianity teaches, around which the Roman Catholic Church developed the (man-made) Christianity religion. The Nicene Creed that was the initial Rule or Dogma that was used for the new Christian religion. However, God in Isaiah 29:13 called it "a human rule" that HE clearly didn't agree with.

A third important 'event' but of lesser importance is shown in the light green oval to the right wherein we learn that God expelled Satan from Paradise simultaneously with Adam and Eve. God negates what's written in the Book of Revelation Chapter 12:7-9, which - as we've learned – is untrue. It's written that Satan and his angels had a war in heaven against the archangel Michael and his angels and ended up being thrown out from heaven. Satan wasn't an angel and God expelled him simultaneously with Adam and Eve. Nothing agrees.

Jesus received God's original Monotheistic Religion for him to institute. Changing it into a Trinity Religion as was done later on, made it a pagan religion, a change with abysmal consequences for every Christian. It's so, because, since God hadn't been involved in the formation of the Christian trinity religion, as we shall learn, the religion, its founders (the new Roman Catholic and the Greek Orthodox churches, as well as anybody involved) and its believers were taken away from God. Guess by who? Yes, by Satan! God had said it very clearly 'only HE was (is) to be worshipped.'

God authored the Qur'an as His new Law, replacing any and all His Scriptures, for the reason that they had been changed (corrupted) as HE told His Prophet Jeremiah in chapter 8:8.

One of the most important implications of the man-made (not by God) change from the existing Monotheistic religion was that extensive parts of what His Apostles had written in their Gospels about Jesus, their teacher, God's unique Prophet, especially the ideas of who he was, was altered so as to agree with the new Christian Trinity (three godheads) religion.

Another, even more important change that had been made was the eradication of the most important of God's Ten Commandments. It had to be done, because they didn't (don't) fit the Christian Trinity religion, negating what God had taught to his Prophet Moses and again to Jesus – that HE is the only Living God (the Creator of everything), who is to be worshipped.

In the New Testament, as mentioned before, Matthew 19:18, Mark 10:13-16 and Luke 18:18-30 we have learned that the most important Commandments as God taught them to Moses in the Book of Exodus 20:1-17, wherein HE begins saying *"I am the Lord .... Worship no God but me,* have been eradicated."

This is of immeasurable consequence for all Christians, but principally for those who teach and preach it, i.e., the priesthoods. This is so because the consequence of any change made to words of God, is a mayor sin *'that will take the sinner to Hell'.*

I'll provide detailed information of the many things that lead up to the change of God's religion. I have mentioned Satan several times, and it is Vitally Important to bring him into the picture to provide clearcut evidence of his existence and how he deceived the Christian Priesthood away from God.

As we've learned, the best way for Satan to deviate people away from God is by getting them to adopt religions that aren't of God that deviate millions of people, as they uselessly and to their detriment worship 'inexistent' gods, mainly Jesus; and the virgin Mary, whose only virtue – although a very important one - was that of giving birth to a unique human being and future Prophet by the name of Jesus. Then, there are the countless Saints created by the Catholic Church, as Satan surely whispered to the Popes to do that don't exist.

The change of the texts in the gospels and other in the New Testament was influenced or manipulated by Satan – because, who else - would induce ideas into the minds of the early Roman Catholic Priesthood. Satan, the master of deceit, knew what to whisper into their minds what he wanted them to believe – such as, most importantly - that Jesus was the son of God and thus a god; taking most of His slaves (God calls us, mankind, His slaves, not His children) away from *Him*, as he had promised to do after the creation.

In the Qur'an, that was authored by God, HE says repeatedly that HE has no son. HE also says, "*Don't say trinity*".

Based on all of this the question is, what really happened to Jesus, around whom so much has been written? Most of which is false.

It's said about Jesus that he originated Christianity. Well, yes and no. How come you ask? Yes, while he lived, he originated the introduction of the Monotheistic (one only God) religion that God had given to him that became known as Christianity that lasted close to three-hundred years.

The Christianity that was instituted from the year 325AD - namely the Trinity Christianity – has nothing in common with the teachings of the religion that God had given to him, the same HE had given to Moses that teaches that HE is the only God.

I was a Christian for most of my life, until I made my findings as the result of my in-depth investigation related to the ancient End-of-Time Prophecies of God. It opened my eyes in regards to who Jesus was, not the son of God, but a Unique Prophet, who

God created in ways akin to how HE created Adam, i.e., without a father.

In the following, I'm sharing with you what I learned from my investigations and especially what God has revealed in the Qur'an.

The Book of Revelation - supposedly written by John (which John? I ask), while he was exiled on the Island of Patmos in Greece, opened up myriads of question-marks because of how it's written. I found it to have a mishmash of issues, before I realized why it was written in such a way, that we shall look into as we move on.

The Qur'an, which I began to read, out of pure interest, some thirty years ago, is a remarkable Book, which I bring up and quote extensively in my previously mentioned Book.

I found that Revelations, which God had made in the Jewish Bible and in the Book of Revelation are mentioned in the Qur'an, frequently with much more detail. It's vitally important to know that the Qur'an was authored by God. We have learned that God transferred the Qur'an verbally through His archangel Gabriel to the Prophet Mohammad, whom he met more than twenty thousand times, as recorded. Christian leaders teach their congregations that the Qur'an is of demonic origin to make them to stay away from it. It's a monstruous lie that will be severely punished, as God reveals in the Qur'an.

You ask why the Qur'an came to be? First of all, it's important to know - as mentioned - that God was the Author of the Qur'an.

There's no doubt that the Qur'an – that contains the LAWS of God – came to be as the result of the many texts that had been corrupted in the TORAH in the Jewish Bible and the corrupted narratives in the New Testament as well as in the Book of Revelation.

This Book is about Jesus and Christianity. Soon after that I began writing it, I found quite to my surprise that in the Qur'an, God, Allah in Arabic – refers to Jesus in numerous Chapters, describing who he was and also what he was not, which is remarkable. It differs, as mentioned, from texts in the New Testament and in the Book of Revelation.

In the following Chapter, I will discuss what God reveals in the Qur'an about the birth of Jesus that's completely different from what's written in the New Testament.

This Book and my Book, 'The Unfortunate Destiny of our Planet and Us' serves as a warning to Christians of the need to change your ways of being and your belief in God. Whatever you have been taught was influenced by Satan, who wants us all to go to Hell, to burn and suffer there for all eternity. You want that to happen? God doesn't care what you do.

I say this, if I'm too busy and don't take time to worship the only God and ask him for guidance, how can I expect Him to take time for me?

Stop whatever you are doing and open your minds. Is it better to worship an inexistent son of God, of whom HE never mentioned one Word, since there isn't one? I say without hesitation. No!

Keep on doing it, and you and your soul are lost, and will suffer greatly in your next life in the hereafter, for all eternity, as the result of your own doings, without afterthought.

CHAPTER 1

ABOUT THE VIRGIN MARY AND THE BIRTH OF JESUS, AS GOD DESCRIBES IT IN CHAPTER 19 MARY/MARIAM, IN THE QUR'AN. IT'S A REMARKABLE, COMPLETELY DIFFERENT STORY THAT'S VITALLY IMPORTANT TO KNOW.

It is important to learn that after the chapter about Mary and the birth of Jesus, God never mentions her again. God doesn't mention even one word about Joseph. That's how important they were.

The Story of Mary and the birth of Jesus - as God tells it in the Qur'an - is completely different from what's written in the New Testament in the Christian Bible.

In the story of his birth narrated by the new Roman Catholics in the New Testament it's said that angels and shepherds were in attendance to celebrate the birth of Jesus that took place in an animal stable. Those who invented the story, that included angels, as I see it, where trying to accommodate the new Christian ideas wherein it's stated that Jesus is the son of God.

It's of great importance, as I've mentioned several times to know that, in the Qur'an God refutes time after time that HE has a son and that Jesus would have said that he was His son.

The All-knowing, All-seeing God tells His story in the Qur'an to put in place what happened with Mary, before she gave birth to the baby Jesus, and occurrences immediately after his birth. God doesn't say even one word about a husband, because he is unimportant.

Mary was a young woman whom God had chosen a long time before, because of her purity, to give birth while being a virgin, making her the mother of Jesus, a human being. I say, the purest human ever having walked on earth.

In the following, a few parts of the story of Mary, as God tells it in the Qur'an in Chapters 3 named Ali Imram (Mary's father), and in Chapter 19 called Maryam (Mary). Therein, God tells the story of what really happened to the Virgin Mary, relative to the birth of Jesus.

In Qur'an 19:17-26 God reveals that HE sent to Mary His archangel Gabriel (Jibril in Arabic), who appeared before her in her room, in the form of a man. When Gabriel approached Mary, she asked for the protection of God.

Gabriel told her he was a messenger from God to tell her that she was going to give birth to a son, whose name would be Jesus.

Gabriel told Mary that Jesus would speak to the people from his crib and that he would be of the righteous. Gabriel telling Mary that Jesus would speak from the crib, sounds incredible.

She answered that no man had touched her, nor was she impure, so how could she have a child?

Gabriel responded that the LORD creates what HE wills. HE decrees a matter and by saying - **'Be'** - it becomes. The subject has already been decided. It's easy for God to do anything HE pleases.

Gabriel told Mary that God was going to teach Jesus to write and give him wisdom. HE would teach him the TORAH and the Gospel, and would be a messenger for the Children of Israel.

Mary felt awkward, because she wanted to avoid being seen carrying a baby without having a husband. In the Jewish Society, such a situation was punished by the stoning until death.

From Qur'an 19:22-24 we learn that when her time was nearing, Mary left her home alone. She went to the Bethlehem Valley, close to Jerusalem. There, she found a place (in what must have been an oasis) that faced east where she put up a partition so that she wouldn't be seen.

An angel appeared to Mary telling her that the LORD had *provided a* stream of water *at her feet where they stood. She needed only to shake the trunk of the date-palm-tree where they stood, whereupon fresh ripe dates would fall to her.* I'm sure God made those dates to be the most nutritious and tastiest for Mary.

The angel went on telling Mary that if anybody approached her, she should say that she had vowed a fast unto the Most Benevolent God, why she couldn't speak to anybody.

There was no husband with her when Jesus was born, as the story goes in the New Testament. There was no stable and no angels or shepherds. Why is that?

As you surely have realized from the foregoing, Mary was out in the open giving birth. The only cover she had was that of the date-palm trees. From this we realize that it must have been summer and thus warm. We don't know the day when Jesus was born, but from this revelation of God, we know for sure that it wasn't in December, when it's cold, as the Christian story goes.

At last, Mary conceived the baby. In Qur'an 19:27-28, God reveals the remarkable things that happened when Mary (alone – as mentioned before, no Joseph is mentioned by God) brought the baby to her people, carrying him in a basket.

We learn that when Mary was questioned about the baby by her relatives, she made a gesture towards the baby in the basket.

Her people asked Mary how they could talk to a newborn baby in his crib.

What God reveals in Qur'an 19:30-33 goes beyond belief, when the baby talked, which is one more proof of the remarkable powers of God, who made it happen.

Baby Jesus told Mary's relatives that he was a slave of God, Who had given him the Scripture (TORAH and Gospel) and that he was going to be a Prophet.

Jesus said many more things and I recommend that you read what he said. If you don't own the Qur'an, you can easily go in on the Internet and check out what the newborn Jesus said.

In Qur'an 19:34 God says that such was Jesus, the son of Mary (Maryam). It is a true statement about him, about who Jesus really was (but not His son).

Jesus, speaking from his crib, as a new-born baby, was a miracle of format that avoided Mary the accustomed punishment. You may recall that the angel Gabriel had told Mary when he announced Jesus to her that "Jesus would speak to the people from His crib".

God's story about Mary and the circumstances around her birth of Jesus, as we've learned, is markedly different from the one in the New Testament in the Christian Bible? How could it be? Wherefrom did those stories of the angels and the shepherds come from? Without a doubt Satan was there inducing his ideas into the minds of the new Christian priesthood, in charge of changing the original texts to conform with the new man-made scripts for the new Christian trinity in the New Testament Bible.

We need to know that in the Qur'an, God refutes that HE has a son and that Jesus would have said that he was His son!

Jesus was a unique human individual (as he was narrated to be), and pure. God made sure that Jesus didn't inherit a genetic build-up that for all other humans includes wickedness and (inherited) corrupted minds, et al.

God's story provides the evidence that Jesus wasn't born in December because it's cold then. In such a scenario (the Christian one) shepherds (God doesn't mention any, which means that there were none present) couldn't have been there if Jesus had been born in December. And how come they weren't there with Mary. And where were the angels, and the three Kings?

The 25th of December was an old pagan holiday that was picked by Pope Julius I in the year 350 AD, to be celebrated as the birth-date of Jesus as well. The adoption of this date, when the Winter Solstice was celebrated - as is believed - was made by the Pope to apiece the Roman pagan population. But by celebrating Jesus' birth-date on the same date when they celebrated their different gods, Christianity became just another Roman pagan cult; 'all in the same boat', 'sinking together', so to say.

The reason to bring this up is that the Story of Mary and Jesus in the New Testament describe situations that couldn't have happened. Jesus is of great importance in both Judaism and Islam - as a Prophet.

I want to take you as far back as to about three-thousand and three-hundred years ago, about twelve-hundred years before the birth of Jesus. I'm doing this because I'm convinced that when God told Moses to tell the people (Deuteronomy 18:18), that HE would *send them* (the Jewish people) *a prophet 'like you* Moses', *who would be from their own* (Jewish) people;" HE had already '*defined*' who that future Prophet was going to be.

But not only that, God doubtless had also checked out and made His choice of the parents of the woman - Mary – and of her forefathers, *to be in the lineage of David*, who would give birth to Jesus, a unique Prophet.

The unique semen that God implanted into the Virgin Mary, was free from impurities (evil, wickedness et al) manifested in the corrupted genetics of humankind.

HE made it up in His mind; then when the time came, HE commanded semen with special characteristics to **'Be'** in the uterus of Mary.

By creating Jesus, as the unique human being he was, but not His son; God made him inimitable from all other human beings; unaffected by the hereditary evil created and carried by humanity, impossible for Satan to affect.

In regards to Jesus, as we've learned because of the extraordinary way how God made him to be born - without a human father - it's evident that God prepared that unique individual and Prophet, long before he was born, for a unique future mission and destiny.

Again, it's up to you if you want to believe this or not. My purpose in writing this Book is to give you the opportunity to change your belief in God and worship Him in your hearts, and believe in His Ten Commandments.

If you do, you'll please God!

If you don't, you'll please Satan.

It's your pick!

CHAPTER 2

WHAT GOD REVEALS ABOUT JESUS IN THE QUR'AN VERSUS WHAT'S WRITTEN IN THE NEW TESTAMENT

As we know, as mentioned, Jesus was a unique individual in many ways, beginning with his birth without a father, which is mentioned in the Christian New Testament as well as in the Qur'an. But that's just about the only thing that agrees in both Books, wherein it's written that God's Archangel Gabriel appeared to Mary and announced to her that she was going to have a son by the name of Jesus.

It is of the essence that we talk about Jesus and matters that occurred as the result of how his name and persona became used. There's not the least doubt that the original stories about Jesus, written by his apostles, disciples and other, became heavily manipulated by Satan to make mankind to fall away from God.

You may think what you want about Satan; what is so awful with him is that he has nothing to win by making man fall. It's his unrelenting hatred against us – '*the Children of Adam*' - which keeps him working day and night 24/7 to take us away from 'the Way' of God.

Before getting into the matter of the persona of Jesus, let's again for a moment go to Deuteronomy 18:16-20, from the time of the Prophet Moses - active in the 14th-13th Century BC - when God through him mentioned the appearance of a future Prophet.

This is – without a doubt – one of the most significant revelations of God; it's so because therein we learn that God told Moses that HE would send the Jewish People a Prophet (in some future) who would be "*like you Moses*".

Moses gathered the Jewish people (after they had been taken out from Egypt under his leadership, heavily supported by God).

Pay close attention to what God told Moses that he was to tell the Jewish people.

Moses told the Jewish people that o*n the day when they were gathered at* the foot of *Mount Sinai, they had asked not to hear the LORD speak again or to see His blazing presence inside clouds anymore because they were afraid that it would cause them to die.*

Moses told the people that based on their request, the LORD had accepted what they had asked for, which HE said, 'was wise'. HE, God, told Moses that HE would send them a prophet, who was going to be like Moses, from among their own people. God was going to tell him what to say and he was going to tell the people everything that God commanded him to say, speaking in His name.

I don't intend to continue with this matter, but recommend that you enter the Internet and look up the Book of Deuteronomy 18:16-20 in the Jewish Bible (Old Testament) to learn more.

God's promise is remarkable! The question then that begs to be answered is - who was that Prophet?

There came many Jewish Prophets after Moses, but none who came close to being **'like Moses'** – other than Jesus - who was 'from among their own (Jewish) people' while nowhere in the TORAH (the Old Testament), one that resembled what God told Moses.

Here we have 'black on white' that God promised that HE would send the people "*a Prophet*". Why did God never mention to His prophets that HE had a son? HE didn't, quite simply because He doesn't have a son. Therefore, the Prophet that God promised Moses was Jesus, a Jew.

Muslims regard Jesus to be a Prophet, (as they view Moses) because that's what God has revealed in the Qur'an. The Jewish people believe likewise that both were Prophets. Christians, on the other hand have been made to believe that Jesus was the son of God. It's a monstrous lie that's affecting Christians in the most horrible way into Eternity.

In order to have a son God would have had to 'conceive' him with a 'consort' by making her 'pregnant'? Did you ever hear about God having a consort (a wife)? No, HE didn't/doesn't have one.

Then, a vital question to ask is, why God would need a son? But, the most overwhelmingly important question is, as indicated above; why didn't HE disclose to His Jewish Prophets – to whom HE revealed so many important matters - that HE had a son?

The answer is, because how would God disclose that HE had a son HE didn't have.

The truly overpowering question of all, as I view it is - given that HE never disclosed to His Prophets that HE had a son – from where did such an improbable idea come that Jesus was the son of God?

But, most important of all is that the only one who could with certainty disclose the existence of a son, is God. Any human being who comes up with such an idea, as it occurred, was undoubtedly given it by Satan to invent such an outrageous idea.

The idea that was created that Jesus was the son of God happened sometime in the early part of the third Century AD in Alexandria, Egypt. The Christian priesthood, as we've learned, had been without a spiritual leader since the parting of Jesus. The teachings that Jesus had imparted long time before, of a monotheistic religion – in essence the Jewish belief – had kept becoming more and more nebulous.

Surrounded, as the Christian priesthood was by pagan cults, and predominantly the Egyptian Isis trinity cult, it wasn't strange that they became swayed in the original religion - established by Jesus - of *a 'Monotheistic One and Only God'*.

After studying the subject of how Jesus was made to be the son of God, we realize that making Jesus into a man-made god was a victory of gargantuan dimension for Satan. This is so because making Jesus into the son of God and thus a god - who Christians worship – in competition with the only living God - is a great tragedy for Christianity.

Why I say this is because Christianity became a religion that worships an inexistent (man-made) god; at the same time that the only God has been placed in a 'secondary' place.

Before going on, it's worth the while to be philosophical and make a few annotations about this remarkable individual. First of all is the fact, as we learn in both the New Testament and the

11

Qur'an that Jesus was specially 'created' by God, Who 'made' him to be born without a father, using a human virgin mother, the virgin Mary.

In Qur'an 19:88-93 God reveals what the Prophet Muhammad said in regards to this matter, which is that *those who say that God has begotten a son preach a terrible lie of such dimension that as we learn from what's said in the Qur'an, the heavens might crack, the earth collapse and the mountains become dust at attributing a son to God. It is inappropriate to say that God has a son (because HE has none).*

The fact that the Christian high-level Priests - the bishops – decided for God, imposing on him, that HE has a son – that's untrue - is one of the worst sins ever committed against God; that will cost Christians greatly in the hereafter!

In Qur'an 19:37-38 God declares that it will be misery for all *disbelievers (those who believe that Jesus is His son) who will be punished on Judgment Day, when they will learn the truth. On that Day, they will be able to see very clearly - what they engineered for themselves - when they appear before God!*

In Qur'an 19:39-40 God tells Muhammad to forewarn them (the people/mankind) about *'the Day of Intense Regret'* when this matter is going to be dealt with. At this moment they are paying no heed and do not believe. Ultimately, all things will perish and all human beings will appear in front of God.

Before continuing, I want to bring up an issue that's of fundamental importance for Christians to know. Please refer to the Chart on page 10. In Qur'an 2:37 God declares that HE accepted Adams and Eve's repentance (forgiving them), but punished them for disobeying Him, expelling them (and Satan, who God revealed HE expelled at the same time) from Paradise.

Most important of all, is there was nothing 'pending' that would require an 'Offer Lamb'.

What the Roman Catholic Church came to call the *'Original Sin'* upon which Christianity was based - was invented by them - since it isn't mentioned by God anywhere in the Book of Genesis or in the Qur'an.

In addition, in explicit revelations of God in Qur'an 4:157, HE reveals that the Jewish Priesthood said that they had killed Jesus. But HE declares that *'Jesus was neither crucified nor killed'*. God reveals that *'they (*the Jews*) thought they did, because the matter had been made dubious to them* (by God).' **Check out the *'Central part'* of the Chart on page 11 to which I shall return.**

The new Roman Catholic priesthood got the idea from the Jews, who thought and believed that Jesus had been crucified and died and also that he resurrected (something that as we shall find out didn't happen). Those ideas that shaped the Christian religion have had far-reaching consequences for all Christians to our days.

Without a doubt, it was one of Satan's greatest victories in tricking the then (in the year 325AD) new Christian (of pagan origin) priesthood and their followers away from God.

God reveals that HE 'took' Jesus up to heaven, to avoid that he should unnecessarily suffer a pointless terrible death for a reason that didn't exist.

But the Jewish priesthood had been made (acted upon by God, as revealed in the Qur'an) to believe that it was Jesus they did away with. As we shall learn, it was somebody else who was crucified and died.

God caused Jesus to disappear because of what the Jewish Priesthood - led by the High Priest Caiaphas - were doing with Jesus to take him out of the way (because they were afraid of him and viewed him as a threat).

But, how could such a thing occur? How could then the story in the New Testament be so wrong? We shall take a close look at this and other matters related to Jesus.

CHAPTER 3

WHAT WAS IT THAT REALLY HAPPENED WHEN THE JEWISH PRIESTHOOD WENT AFTER JESUS TO KILL HIM?

As we learned, what God – who knows everything - has revealed in the Qur'an relative to Jesus, doesn't coincide with what's written in the Gospels of Matthew, Mark, Luke, and John in the Christian New Testament. In view of this – which points towards heavy re-writing of the original texts in the four Gospels and other - I decided to make in-depth research to find out what had really happened.

According to what's written in the New Testament, Jesus was betrayed by his disciple Judas Iscariot, who sold Jesus, for thirty silver coins to the Jewish priesthood.

As I've found out, what's written in the New Testament is incorrect. What really happened, according to the Qur'an, in part, but mainly to the Gospel of Barnabas (an amazing book that brings out the clear truth), was that after that Judas Iscariot got the money from Caiaphas, he took the soldiers to where Jesus was staying with his Apostles at the home of a friend, outside of Jerusalem.

Judas hurried and was well ahead of the soldiers when he reached the house and entered. Because the apostles were asleep, Judas called out the name of Jesus. The apostles woke up and went downstairs to see what was going on.

Moments before, according to Barnabas Gospel, God had acted taking away Jesus. HE had ordered His four archangels Gabriel, Michael, Raphael and Uriel to take away Jesus. They carried him, taking him out through a window and up to heaven, where he was to stay until the end of time.

When Judas arrived, Jesus was gone. According to the Gospel of Barnabas, God in no time changed Judas to look like Jesus and to sound like him, when he talked. So, when the apostles saw Judas they said, Master why are you talking like that? The next thing happening was that the soldiers entered and immediately seized Judas thinking that he was Jesus.

Judas began to protest asking that they let go of him. Didn't they see that he was Judas, what was the matter with them, and so on. But the soldiers, convinced that he was Jesus, held him by the arm, and wouldn't let go. He was told to shut up and stop trying to make them think he was another person.

They all left and headed back to Jerusalem, where they handed Judas, who they thought was Jesus, over to the priesthood. As is written, the chief-priests and the Sanhedrin (the Council) were looking for evidence against Jesus so that they could have him be put to death.

But they hadn't been able to find any, though they arranged for witnesses to come forward and provide testimony. Finally, two men had come forward declaring that Jesus had *said that he was able to destroy the temple of God and rebuild it in three days.*

Caiaphas is said to have stood up and asked Jesus, actually Judas, if he wasn't *going to answer to the testimony that the men were bringing against him.* But Judas continued protesting saying that he was Judas and not Jesus and to let him go, which caused Caiaphas to go against Judas, telling him all kinds of things, believing he was Jesus.

Jesus, well Judas, was told to answer *under oath by the living God, if he was the Son of God, the Messiah.* But Judas, who didn't have a clue of what was happening, continued protesting and didn't answer.

The Jewish priests thereupon spit in the face of Judas and struck him with their fists. Others slapped him and said, 'Let's hear a prophecy, Messiah. Tell us who hit you?'

From this story, we can clearly observe the great influence that Satan had and has over conceited people, not because he has any real power, as God made clear in the Qur'an, but because people fall for the ideas he implants in their minds.

Early the next day, Jesus (Judas) was taken to Pontius Pilate, the Roman Governor who began to question Jesus, rather Judas, without getting anywhere, while Judas was trying to get the Governor to understand that he wasn't Jesus.

Since Pilate didn't find any fault with him, and following the established custom, he turned to the crowd and asked, who they *wanted him to set free, Jesus Barabbas, a criminal, or Jesus called the Messiah?*

Pilate was doubtlessly aware that the Jewish Priesthood had handed Jesus over to him because they wanted him to make the decision to have him killed.

While this had been going on – as written – the Jewish priests and elders had been talking with the Jewish crowd on the scene, convincing the people to request from Pilate that he free Barabbas and that Jesus be put to death.

The result of how the Jewish High priests and elders were instigating the people - must be viewed as 'subversive criminal activity' against Jesus - was therefore that when Pilate asked the crowd, who they wanted him to set free.

The crowd shouted, 'Free Barabbas!'

Pilate then asked them what they wanted him to do with Jesus called the Messiah, 'Crucify him!' the crowd shouted.

Pilate then asked the people what crime Jesus had committed.

Instigated as they were by the Jewish Priesthood – that Jesus was a dangerous criminal, the crowd continued shouting that he be crucified.

When Pilate saw that it was useless to go on, he took some water, washed his hands in front of the crowd, and said that he wasn't *responsible for the death of Jesus! It was their doing!*

The crowd shouted back, 'Let the responsibility for his death fall on us and on our children!' They really had no idea of the terrible thing they were doing, how it would affect the Jewish people in the future.

But, in reading the Qur'an 4:157-158, I found a revelation of God - to which all Christians - need to pay close attention. The reason to say this is because the 'scenario', 'circumstances and the 'outcome' that God revealed about what happened with Jesus, are different to what's described in the New Testament because it affects Christianity in its Core.

In the Qur'an God says that the Jews *believed that they killed Jesus, the Messiah, the son of Mary. But, what God says, as mentioned, is that they did not kill Jesus, nor was he crucified.*

God reveals that somebody else *was made to* the Jews *to resemble Jesus.*

In the Qur'an God says that for certain, they did not crucify Jesus, but that the matter had been made dubious to them (to all who were present).

The Prophet Mohammad tells us what happened. *'Nay! The fact is that God brought Jesus up to Him.'*

These are extraordinary revelations of God, and HE is the Wise, the All-knowing, the All-mighty and All-seeing.

Understand that the intention of the Jewish establishment to kill Jesus (God's Prophet) counts as if they had killed him.

I want to stop here for a moment and again refer to the Book of Deuteronomy 18:8 wherein God mentioned to Moses that HE was going to send the Jewish People a Prophet like Moses. This event occurred close to the end of the Ministry and life of Moses, around Three-thousand-three-hundred years ago; about Thirteen-hundred years before the birth of Jesus, the apparent Prophet mentioned by God. What I want to bring into the scenario is that given that God knew who that Prophet was going to be - in addition to many things, HE knew what was going to happen to that Prophet.

As we know, God made (created) Jesus to be born from a Virgin, Mary, without a husband. We know this for certain, because it's written in both The New Testament and the in the Qur'an. God knew, when HE told Moses about that future Prophet, who was to be born from a woman on the lineage of King David.

What you need to know is that given that God knew all about His promised Prophet, there's no doubt in my mind that HE knew about Caiaphas and what he was going to try to do to Jesus. And I say that why would God let Caiaphas get it his way? For what reason?

Now, think about this. There was absolutely no reason for God to let the Jewish people kill His Unique Prophet. So, everything that had happened to that point, when Pilatus was about to hand over Jesus, the Messiah, hadn't caused any damage to Jesus.

It's more than obvious they didn't realize how distanced they had become from God, their 'Benefactor'! It was in fact, a for the Jewish People terribly fatidic circumstance.

Before going on I want to bring in what God said to His Prophet Jeremiah 11:11 about the Covenant, sometime in the early part of the sixth century B.C., as follows.

Jeremiah wrote, "The LORD said to me, '*Listen to the terms of the covenant. Tell the people of Judah and of Jerusalem that I, the LORD God of Israel, have placed a curse on everyone who does not obey the terms of this covenant.*'"

"*It is the covenant I made with their ancestors when I brought them out of Egypt. I told them to obey me and to do everything that I had commanded. I told them that if they obeyed, they would be my people and I would be their God. Then I would keep the promise I made to their ancestors that I would give them the rich and fertile land which they now have.*"

Through Jeremiah 11:11 the LORD God also said, "*So now, I, the LORD, warn them* (the Jewish people) *that I am going to bring destruction on them, and they will not (be able to) escape.*"

This is remarkable, isn't it? Because this explains why it hasn't gone well for the Jewish people.

Per the 2016 world population count, there were just over Fourteen Million Jewish people, of a Total World population of Seven and a half Billion, which translates into just under 0.16%.

In 1939 the Jewish World population was close to Seventeen Million. Through the 2nd World War, they became decimated to Eleven Million, a reduction of 35%. According to the revelations they made themselves pre-destined for this fate.

In the Jewish Bible, the Lord God provided a host of – as I view it – very negative revelations relative to the rebellious behavior of the Jewish people against Him. It gives the idea of why it has gone bad for them. God obviously knew what was going to happen, but wanted anyhow to give them an opportunity.

I'm convinced that what they did (intended to do) to God's Unique Prophet Jesus, weighs especially heavy against them in the 'balance', something that has been fatidic for them.

Something else that weighs heavy against the Jewish people(s) is revealed by the Only Living God in the Qur'an 3:187-189 that reads (a repeat), "When God made the covenant with those who were given the Book (The TORAH - the Book that God called His LAW), HE told them to spread (to share) His teachings of the Book with mankind and not to conceal them; but they (the Jews) cast it (the immutable orders of God) behind their backs.

CHAPTER 4

FROM THE QUR'AN WE LEARN THAT SATAN, OUR SWORN ENEMY, PROMISSED TO GOD HE WOULD MAKE MAN FALL AWAY FROM HIM?

- HE CERTAINLY HAS DONE AN OUTSTANDING JOB -

In *the Qur'an, God reveals that HE created His angels from pure white light. We also learn that HE* didn't bestow them a *'free will'*, therefore, it's impossible for an angel to turn against God and disobey Him, as the Roman Catholic Church tells it.

We learn that God taught Adam the names of all angels. HE presented Adam to the angels and Jinn and told Adam to t*ell them their names.* When Adam had told the angels their names, God ordered the angels and Jinn, *to bow down to Adam* (to show their respect for his knowledge). All bowed down, except a Jinn, by the name Iblis who refused to bow to Adam.

I say, how many of us don't commit errors - over and over - in our arrogance that takes us away from God.

God asked Iblis what had prevented him from prostrating himself to one who HE had created with His Hands? Was he too proud to prostrate to Adam or did he think he could do as he pleased?

Iblis responded that he was better than Adam, for the reason that God had created him from smoke-free fire, while HE created Adam from dirt.

We observe that Iblis looked down on God's creation of the man who was made from dirt.

God ordered Iblis – the new become Satan, also known as the Devil - to get out from His presence, which made Satan an outcast. God told Iblis that His curse was on him till the Day of Resurrection (the Day when mankind and Jinn will be brought to God for Final Judgment).

We learn that Iblis (Satan) despite, of what had happened, kept being respectful to God, when he asked to be given 'respite till the Day of Resurrection.'

It's evident that since Iblis – Satan - directed himself to God with respect, there's no doubt that he knew '*his place*'!

God responded that Satan was reprieved (this means that God 'granted Satan a stay before his punishment went into effect'), until the Day of Resurrection.

It is important to understand that Iblis, the new become Satan was condemned but was allowed by God to continue '*to be around*' until the Day of Resurrection.

This has been (is) to the detriment of mankind.

The following statements made by Satan to God - and God's response to him – in accordance to the Qur'an, are of paramount importance that every human being gets to know.

Satan answered to God (respectfully) that since he had been given respite, he was going to mislead all human beings except *'His chosen slaves'* (those who believe in God without a doubt).

Satan declared to God that he would lay in wait on the human beings. He would ensnare them and make them *fall away from 'The Straight Way' of God.* He would come upon them from in-front and from behind, from their right and their left. Satan told God that HE would find out that most of them would be unthankful to Him and that not many would be left on His *'Straight Way'.* In other words, we (human beings) are ungrateful to God because we don't realize that we have Him to thank for the life we have.

This is vitally important to know and understand. The new become Satan became man's instant enemy (it was because of man that God cursed Iblis/Satan). Satan wowed to God that he was going to go after the human beings – His slaves - and destroy all those who weren't God's *'chosen slaves'.*

God told Satan that he would have no authority over His slaves (mankind), except those who followed him (Satan) [non-believers, polytheists (those who believe in and worship several gods), criminals and evil-doers]. Hell was the place that was guaranteed for them all.

God declared to Satan that HE *would fill Hell with him* [Iblis/Satan] *and all those who followed him.*

This is yet another (most) critically important revelation of God, wherein HE told Satan that HE (God) allowed Satan to go after the human beings as he pleased, without restraints – until the end of time.

CHAPTER 5

THE ILL-FATED CHRISTIAN BISHOPS FIRST ECUMENICAL CONFERENCE IN NICAEA, TURKEY, IN 325AD

REASONS FOR WHY THE CHRISTIAN BISHOPS FIRST ECUMENICAL CONFERENCE CAME TO HAPPEN.

Why do I call it '*ill-fated*'? It is, as we shall learn, for the reason that the changes that were introduced to the Monotheistic Religions of Jesus, was like shooting a torpedo into a ship, making it to explode and sink to the bottom of the Ocean, taking practically all the people onboard with it.

It's of the essence to know that the issue of *Jesus personae was* debated extensively by the newly formed Christian priesthoods of the time, pagan converts.

We need to understand that the Christian priesthoods in all probability, were unfamiliar with the Jewish Bible and thus the Revelations of God and most importantly His Commandments.

The Jewish people kept their distance to the Christians (against what God had told them to do). I say it was also because the Jewish Bible was written in the Hebrew, Greek and Aramaic languages that were foreign to them.

Before moving on it's important to know that there existed numerous pagan *Trinity Cults*, that originated from ancient Babylon and Assyria that moved away after that God changed the only language, as punishment for the wickedness of the people.

The Egyptian Isis cult focused on the celebration of the mysteries of the death and the resurrection of Osiris. The story in brief: The goddess, Isis, was the consort of Osiris who was murdered and cut in pieces. Isis, the story goes, recovered the scattered parts of his body and restored him to life. Osiris became the king of the dead and their son Horus the king of the living.

Isis, it was thought, had the power over life and death and could resurrect her followers in the same manner that she was said to have brought her husband Osiris back to life. As the myth of Isis and Osiris grew, the Isis cult became more and more popular and displaced other cults.

It goes without saying that the Christians of the time were strongly influenced by the pagan cults around them. The cult that was of special consequence for how Christianity developed as a trinity was doubtless the Egyptian Isis mystical Trinity Cult; it had been adopted by the Romans and became one of the prevailing ones of many pagan cults in the Roman Empire that became popular around the Mediterranean.

The Isis cult is believed to have given origin to Christian mysteries, such as the resurrection of Jesus. The Isis cult also gave rise to numerous Christian symbols, including that of the Madonna and the Child, as pictured by Isis with her son Horus.

The cult of Isis continued to be practiced in the Roman Empire right up to the sixth century AD when it was finally overcome by the man-made Christian trinity religion. The Isis cult 'lived on' in certain esoteric traditions throughout the Middle Ages.

As mentioned before, who Jesus was, was a matter of great contention within the Christian priesthoods that went on for hundreds of years, with strong infighting from all sides.

In Alexandria, Egypt, the Christian Bishop, Alexander, developed a 'thesis' wherein he declared that *"God did the unthinkable when He descended into human flesh and became the man Jesus – his son - taking the burden of our sins"* (what sins? God had forgiven Adam and Eve!). Where did he get that from?

A question of great importance to this Chapter, is who was Alexander? Who was he to say that God had a son? Where did he get it from? How could it be that God hadn't disclosed this to His Jewish Prophets, beginning with Moses. It's obvious HE didn't for the very simple reason that HE didn't have a son

I say that Alexander, who I call *'the Inventor of the son of God and of the Christian trinity'*, knew nothing about God or about His Ten Commandments and all other that HE gave to His Jewish People, which are equally valid for all humankind!

A high-level Christian priest Arius, also in Alexandria, developed another 'thesis' wherein he asserted that *"Jesus was indeed the holiest person who ever lived, but he wasn't by any means the Eternal God of Israel walking the earth in the form of a man"*. Arius had many followers who believed as he did.

The main opposition to Arius and to his ideas came from Alexander, who became his formidable and ferocious opponent. Alexander stated that the ideas of Arius were *"worse than mistaken and enormously destructive.... they were a terrible heresy."*

There isn't the least doubt that Satan involved himself in this matter, since it would lead to the spiritual downfall of myriads of his most hated 'unknowing' adversaries.

The amazing thing was that – thanks to the involvement of Constantine I, the Caesar – Satan's job to make many to fall became easy. It was so because Alexander had already 'fallen' for his 'Jesus-son-of-god' idea and Constantine the pagan Caesar had the power to convert the idea into reality.

With regards to Arius, since he wasn't a Bishop, His 'lesser' status and his ability to reach up to the higher echelons and mainly Constantine, was therefore limited or nil. He couldn't therefore harm the ideas of Satan to destroy the Monotheistic Religion that Jesus had been given by God to put in place.

Despite that Constantine the Great decided to become a Christian in 312AD, he didn't allow for himself to be baptized until on his death-bed twenty-five years later in 337AD. The reason why he waited was because he believed that in that way, he was free to do as he pleased *without committing a sin*.

It shows that Constantine - and the Christian Priesthood counselling him - didn't have a clue about what they were doing.

Know that God's Divine Law of 'Cause and Effect' is always 'In Effect' and doesn't 'show mercy' to anybody.

Caesar Constantine I – closely advised by the unseen Satan - took the lead in the definition of the Christian religion - because of how it was growing within his Empire.

Hosius, a Christian Bishop from Spain was his personal advisor in Rome. Constantine sent Hosius to Alexandria to meet with Alexander and Arius to review their respective ideas. Hosius favoured the ideas of Alexander most probably because he knew that that was what Constantine wanted, thereby committing a heinous sin.

Based on the report of Hosius that favoured the ideas of Alexander – as one could expect - Constantine decided to call the Christian bishops in his Empire to a conference to define the Basics of Christianity in accordance with the ideas of Alexander, 'blessed' by the pagan Caesar Constantine, to be 'the way to go'. It was the First Bishops Council that took place at his Summer Residence in Nicaea (in the vicinity of the City of Iznik in Turkey) in 325AD, where the bishops were held captive.

It's important to know that the priesthood was considered servants of the Caesar, so by virtue of his authoritative presence at the conference, there's no doubt, I say, who it was, who really 'presided' the meeting despite that he didn't involve himself directly.

It's a known fact that the bishops were afraid of Constantine known to be a 'hot-blooded man', so who would dare to go against the 'desires' of the mighty Emperor. He had exiled bishops and other in the past who had opposed him – sending them to remote Countries in the Empire. It could happen again!

What was Constantine's take on this matter? Why was this important to him? He did it because he had realized that Christianity was gaining momentum, growing rapidly despite all persecution and killings. When he decided to accept Christianity, it was to make it part of the existing Roman Society with its pagan cults. It was clearly the decision of a statesman - that had nothing to do with religious conviction. The Head of State did what he believed was best for his Empire.

The Bishop's Council was thus called by Constantine so as to incorporate Christianity to become another religion (cult) of the Roman State, and to avoid creating turmoil with the pagan cults, and especially with the Roman Empire's prevalent Isis trinity cult.

The idea of Bishop Alexander from Alexandria of a religion with a father, a son and a holy spirit – a trinity – was to the liking of Constantine. Such religion would be easy to 'piggyback' onto the popular *Isis trinity cult, as a derivative of the same*. It would be a simple matter of introducing a new name, which wouldn't bother his pagan subjects.

And it didn't bother the Christian bishops who – as mentioned – weren't familiar with the Jewish Bible, for the reasons mentioned before, i.e., it was written in languages they didn't understand. The question is, how many had knowledge of its existence?

I'm convinced that if they had been what God had said and very especially with his Commandments, I assert that the Christian trinity religion wouldn't have come into existence.

God, without a doubt knew a long time before of the Bishops Ecumenical Conference and what would come out of it, as with everything else. But since God had given permission to Satan to go after humankind, as he pleased, HE watched what was happening, knowing that Alexander and all who accepted the new Christian trinity, a false religion, would stand in front of Him on Judgment Day to render accounts of why they had made up and worshiped an inexistent son of His, and not Him, the Only Living God.

The outcome of the Bishops Council was the institution of the man-made and thus pagan Nicene (trinity of gods) Creed that ruled that there is the father god, the son Jesus of the same essence as God (?) and a holy ghost (God made into a second being after Jesus, the god of the Christians).

At this point, I suggest going back to Isaiah 29:13-14, what God said about man-made religions - one of the most terrible sins - a great offence against God affecting mankind.

From this, it's obvious that the bishops – as mentioned - had no knowledge of the Jewish Bible and of God's First and following Commandments. If any of the bishops knew, they were too afraid of the Caesar - that he would retaliate if they went against his desires and exile whoever opposed him to some remote location.

It's clear that it was important for the bishops to please Constantine, the pagan Emperor whom they feared, not realising what they had done against the only living God.

Very curiously, Constantine was baptized by an Arian Priest on his death-bed in 337AD. Was it maybe a late change of mind?

The Nicene Creed from 325 AD was amended at later Councils (the Sirmian Creed in 357, the Rimini-Seleucia Creed in 359 and the Constantinople Creed in 381, to mention a few.) From this, we realize that the matter of who Jesus was really wasn't at all 'cast in concrete'. The status of Christianity was 'man-made', not 'God-given'.

I want to recommend reading the Book: 'When Jesus Became God', by Richard Rubenstein that provides an insightful narrative of his in-depth research (how it all came to happen) at the Bishops Ecumenical conference at Nicaea.

The new Roman Christian Church also adopted religious practices, utensils, rites and other from the pagan cults (we see the Pope, Archbishops and Bishops wearing robes and hats – and the rod, and the staff - similar to those used by pagan cults) into the new man-made Roman Catholic Christian trinity religion.

If the new Roman Christian church had known the Jewish Bible – what God told His Prophets – they would have known that God ordered Moses to stay away from adopting pagan practices, as we learn in the Book Exodus 23:24 and 33 and in

Deuteronomy 12:30, when HE Told him, "... *Make sure you* (the Jews) *don't follow their religious practices* (of the pagans) *because that will be fatal.*" "*Do not worship the LORD in the way they* (the pagans) *worship their gods, for in the worship of their gods they do all the disgusting things the LORD hates.*" And, that's the way how the Christian churches worship – following the adopted pagan practices – that God declared **"will be fatal".**

It's not known exactly when Jesus was born, but most scholars agree that he wasn't born in December. So why is Jesus' birthday celebrated as Christmas on December the 25th? The answer lies in the pagan origins of Christianity and of Christmas, none of which has anything to do with God. In ancient Babylon, the pagan feast of Horus, the invented son of the invented goddess Isis was celebrated on December 25. So, there's again a connection with the Isis trinity cult.

In 350 AD, Pope Julius I (as mentioned before) declared that Christ's birth would be celebrated on December 25. There's little doubt that he was trying to make it as painless as possible for Roman pagans (who remained a majority at that time and especially the followers of the Isis trinity cult) to convert to Christianity, another pagan trinity religion. The new religion was thus made easier to accept knowing that the pagan feasts would not be taken away from them. But it would be of terrible consequence – unknown to future Christians – unacceptable to God.

The Christmas tree is of pagan origin. An example of many: During the Roman celebration of the feast of Saturnalia, pagans decorated their houses with clippings of evergreen shrubs. They also decorated living trees with bits of metal and replicas of Bacchus, the Mythological Greek god of wine and feasts.

As we know, because we live it every Christmas, it has become the largest Commercial Event that exists; completely unrelated to Almighty God, Who has declared that HE has no son!

I say it was one of Satan's absolutely greatest victories and at the same time a tragedy of gigantic proportion and consequences for humanity. It's so because from this religion (the Catholic) emanated so many evil occurrences, affecting so many people in many countries.

One of the worst examples is Latin America, where countless atrocities were committed by the Spanish Catholic Church against its native inhabitants and then ongoing, in the name of God.

The Spanish Inquisition however, takes the price in regards to atrocities committed by the church in the name of God.

And, we see nowadays how so many Catholic pedophile Priests have molested thousands and thousands of innocent young children throughout, mostly boys but also girls. And, we also learn how many of those pedophiles have been covered by their superiors up to the level of Popes.

Is there any forgiveness from God for such a heinous sin? I doubt it. Satan will enjoy the company of them in Hell, where, as I believe, they will have *'a-hell-of-a-time'* together.

The Bishops of the East and of the West took stances in their beliefs that separated them from each other. This gave origin to the separation of Christianity into two new churches the Roman Catholic and Greek Orthodox Churches.

CHAPTER 6

THE NEW, BY THE BISHOPS INVENTED TRINITY RELIGION, WITH AN INEXISTENT SON OF GOD AT THE HEAD, LOST ITS SPIRITUALITY, AS THE RESULT OF WHICH GOD BEGAN TO 'KEEP HIS DISTANCE' LOOKING AT US FROM A DISTANCE, AND HUMANKIND (MOST OF US) LOST ITS BY GOD GIVEN ORIGINAL COURSE.

From the point of view of anybody, you, me and everybody else the Ecumenical Conference at Nicaea, would seem to be just another conference of religious people. But the one in Nicaea was unique since it would have far-reaching future consequences for the future of mankind. It's so because 'the seeds' of a religion became 'planted' through the '*man-made*' Nicene Creed that God obviously didn't '*establish*', and had absolutely no part with.

Worst of all is that the consequences – looking into the distant future - of what was put in place at Nicaea – the new man-made (not of God) Christian trinity religion – would dramatically change the course of how mankind would behave, heavily manipulated by Satan, our untiring Nemesis.

As we've learned, the new religion became defined without 'involving' the only Being in the whole universe Who counts –

namely God. We can be absolutely sure that the bishops, subjects of the pagan Roman Caesar Constantine didn't have the faintest idea of *'inviting'* God to partake in the Conference – making it completely lacking of spirituality. We can also be sure that God maintained a good distance from it all. How come, somebody asks?

At issue is that, as already mentioned, and this is extraordinarily important to have in mind that no consideration was taken to God's Commandments, - especially His First - when the new *'man-made'* *'Creed'* (rule) was *'cast in concrete'*. The new trinity (pagan) religion first and last was clearly defined so as to please and serve the purpose of the emperor Constantine (a pagan until his deathbed), so it would 'mix' in with the multitude of pagan cults that existed in His empire, without consideration to the one and only real God and His requirements, defined in the ten Commandments that HE had given to Moses.

It's obvious that those people had no knowledge of God and His Laws contained in the TORAH; wherein HE provided all His Laws and Commandments and detailed guidelines for how to go about life and the mandatory worship of him; and of how not to worship Him that HE had outlined in detail through Moses. Therefore, they were lost.

For Constantine, the 'Head-of-State' for the Roman Empire, his main concern, as mentioned, was to avoid causing turmoil amongst his pagan subjects for bringing in a new cult.

The *'middle way'* he the Caesar chose, doubtlessly was defined by his desire to keep all his pagan subjects happy, while at the same time pleasing his Christian subjects. One could say that he tried to **'*kill two birds*' with one stone. But God knows not of any *'middle way'*** it's either **'*His Way'*** or it's Not!

35

Jesus was aware of what was going to happen with Christianity, how it would be misled, away from *'God's Narrow Way of Righteousness'* – with the LORD being *'The Only Living God'*. Jesus wanted to make sure there was no misunderstanding about his relationship with God, in what he taught:

Jesus said, (This saying of Jesus is of fundamental importance) Matthew 5:18-19. *"**Remember that as long as the heaven and the earth last, not the least point of the (God's) LAW will be done away with – not until the end of all things. So then, whoever disobeys even the least important of the Commandments and teaches others to do the same, will be least in the Kingdom of heaven (will lose his/her salvation and go to the abyss of perdition, to Hell)"**. Jesus continued saying, "**On the other hand, whoever obeys the LAW** (as God gave it to Moses) **and teaches others to do the same, will be great in the Kingdom of heaven.**"*

The bishops involved in the establishment of the Nicene Creed left a terrible legacy that would deeply affect all future trinity Christians, who helped to take away themselves from the Narrow Way of the Almighty Creator as they were misled – them unknowing – to worship an inexistent god, Jesus, God's Prophet.

I say, poor Christian priests, monks and nuns who were forced to live their lives in celibacy, in seclusion, worshipping – as God calls that god in His Commandments, "A *rival that HE doesn't tolerate.*" And, poor all Christians who were deceived to fall away from the Only Living God.

The later adoptions of Christmas to celebrate the birth of an inexistant 'son of God' 'a god' and the so-called Holy Week when his supposed sufferings and death have been commemorated. There isn't the least doubt that all of that will be punished by God! And especially the Christian priesthoods.

CHAPTER 7

AN UNSEEN INVISIBLE ATTENDANT WAS EFFECTVELY PARTAKING IN THE BISHOPS FIRST ECUMENICAL CONFERENCE

We can be sure that Satan, the '*invisible attendant*', was in effect 'leading' the conference, 'manipulating' the minds of the bishops, the Monotheistic faith having been 'torpedoed' by the continuous attacks of Satan. There isn't the least doubt that Satan was in full control of the minds of the bishops. Furthermore, he had Constantine, the pagan Emperor on his side and the priesthood (servants of Constantine) to reach a final conclusion that was to the satisfaction of Constantine and obviously of Satan the '*unseen attendant*'.

Satan would have preferred that nobody knew about this (my) intrusion. As things stand now it doesn't matter because of all the harm that has already been inflicted on a large portion of mankind. Satan took part as an 'influencer' to all in the conference without being noticed by anybody.

His mission '*to wreck Christianity*', became accomplished through the launch of the man-made Nicene Creed, the one that goes against the LAW of God. Knowing Christianity would be deceived in the future, HE made clear in Isaiah 29:13 that the *people honour Him with (empty) words and not with the heart. He also made clear that worshipping Him without their hearts - are far away from Him – because they teach man-made rules and laws".* Here we learn that God doesn't accept *'religions based on man-made Rules and Laws'*!

The winner = Satan. - The looser = All Christians, current and past!

From the 'man-made' Nicene Creed was born the Roman Christian trinity Church that became split into the Catholic Christian and the Greek Orthodox Church. But, as the result of disagreements along the ages, between the many future leaders and scholars about the definitions of Dogmas and Creeds of 'beliefs' and other, it has resulted in countless new Christian churches or sects.

At this point, I want to bring into the picture former Bishop (Episcopal) John Shelby Spong's Book "*The Sins of Scripture*" (the Christian Bible). Therein he elaborates about many issues in the Bible that in accordance with him are 'wrong'. I agree with some of his assessments but strongly disagree with some other.

The bishop wrote in his book that he "*has a lifetime love affair with the Bible*" and – that he is a "*Church Insider*". He seems to believe that this makes him know religious matters well.

I'm instead an individual dedicated to understanding - with an open mind - the 'Will of God' including His Ten Commandment as HE gave them to His Prophet Moses – that became reduced in the New Testament. Why did it happen? Did God change His mind about His commandments? I say God would never have accepted the changes.

Among many things, Bishop Spong wrote that *"The idea of God speaking to give commandments to the created ones seems somewhat inappropriate in our age."* Well, maybe this is a way to try to get rid of the Commandments of God. I'm convinced that Satan is very happy that the bishop listened to him and adopted his ideas.

One of the former Bishop's best assessments, I think, is where he wrote, *"The Christian story has to change in radical ways."* He goes on writing, *"It would be easier, some say* (Who?), *to start over by building an entirely new religion."*

I totally agree with this assessment of his. The big question is, who would lead such – 'impossible task' - and be followed?

It's impossible for this to happen because there are far too many personal interests involved, the ones that have led to the splitting of Christianity into a myriad of Churches that are mainly used as 'money-makers' (cash-cows). But, as God reveals in the Qur'an, church owners who benefit personally from the Donations from their Parishioners, will be severely punished.

Another consequence of the Nicene trinity Creed - as we've learned - is that it eradicated the First Commandment put in place by God about Himself, that HE is the only God.

Still another consequence of the creation of the Christian trinity religion was, without a doubt, one of the leading reasons for God to create Islam and the Qur'an in the seventh century. In the Qur'an God reveals that Islam was created by Him and that HE is the Author of the Qur'an, the meaning of which HE revealed, as we learned before, is *"The Guidance for mankind"*. So, it isn't only for the Muslims.

The question one makes is why, since the Bible existed, did God establish the Qur'an? God has provided the answer, which is that both the TORAH (read Jeremiah 8:7-9) and the Gospel were changed (through the eradication of vital texts) of His original revelations and did therefore not serve the purpose of providing His guidance for mankind. This is confirmed in Qur'an 6:91.

God created Islam as a pure religion, with the Prophet Mohammad at the head. It has gone through many upheavals. God has said, Qur'an 21:92, *"Verily this brotherhood* (mankind) *of yours is a single brotherhood* (one mankind with Islam at the Centre – my comment) *and I Am your only God, LORD, Almighty Creator, Ruler, Master and Owner of all, therefore, worship Me alone!"*

His First Commandment in Exodus in the Bible God says, 20:2 "I am the LORD your God..." 20:3 *"Worship no god but Me"* (No son god or mother god). It's clear!

Important Prophecy made by the Prophet Mohammad in the Hadith, the Book of his Sayings: (in Sunan al-Tirmidhi Hadith Nbr. 171). *"My Ummah* (the only Islamic Religious Community at his time) *will be fragmented into seventy-three sects, and all of them* (the people who belong to them) *will go to the Hell-fire except one* (his then only existing Sunni Ummah)." This revelation of the Prophet speaks for itself.

Despite this, only those people who stay on God's "Narrow *Right Way"*, who worship only Him, who give to the poor and needy (who God has close to His Heart), can hope for salvation.

All those who behave arrogantly against God, who don't believe and worship Him alone, the Only Living God, who lie, steal, cheat, who behave badly against a fellow man or woman, et al, have no hope of salvation, even if they think so. Also, all Muslims who make their so-called Jihad's and kill innocent people are doomed, independently of what they think, an/or their leaders tell them.

The above Prophecy must be viewed against God's revelations in Qur'an 6:159 wherein HE says, *"Surely those who divide the religion (Islam – but the same is valid for Judaism as well) into sects and identify themselves as being part of a sect, O Muhammad, you have nothing to do with them. Their case will be called into account by God Himself. He will tell them (Muslims, Jews and all other - on 'Judgment Day') what they did wrong."*

In Qur'an 3:105 HE also says, "those *responsible for division (into sects) and arguments (*religious leaders and elders*) will be sternly punished"* (by far, far more - then their followers).

As for peoples of other religions (none named – none forgotten) – who worship a multiplicity of gods represented by a variety of idols or effigies and other, plainly contradict the *Commandments* of the Only Living God, the Creator and therefore the owner of everything. It is evident that they were led away from the *'Right Way'* of the Only living God, the Almighty Creator!

Priests who use their position and the name of God to molest defenceless children and nuns (as has happened) will face God on Judgment Day to stand Trial for their heinous acts, as will every individual who covers up those acts (Nobody to be spared)!

CHAPTER 8

COMMANDMENTS OF GOD THAT WERE ERADICATED
IN THE NEW TESTAMENT

I realize that the heading is odd, but, how could God's important Commandments be eradicated? At issue is what Jesus was attributed to have said according to the New Testament Books of Matthew 19:16-31, Mark 10:17-31 and Luke 18:18-30 where only six of God's Ten Commandments - are identically written, as shown.

The overpowering question then is what happened with God's four foremost Commandments (listed below), obviously the important ones from the perspective of God? '**The ones that matter**'.

How could anyone dare to eliminate them? It's very obvious that God's Monotheistic Commandments that HE had given to his Prophet Moses [For mankind] didn't fit in the newly instituted (325AD) (man-made) Christian trinity religion; so, the priesthood of the then new Roman Catholic Church simply took them out.

They obviously had no idea of what they were doing and its disastrous consequences especially for themselves and for their

Christian followers in any and all of the many future Christian denominations.

When did Jesus mention the Commandments of God? It happened when a young very rich man approached Jesus and said "*What good must I do to earn myself eternal life?*"

Jesus looked at him and responded "**If you want to enter eternal life,** keep the Commandments of God." The rich man was then said to have asked, "Which ones?"

Jesus unquestionably must have told him God's Ten Commandments – beginning with His Foremost ones that follow:

THE TEN COMMANDMENTS OF GOD – are valid for every individual

THESE ARE THE PRINCIPAL FOUR COMMANDMENTS WHEREIN HE DEFFINES WHO HE IS AND HOW HE WANTS TO BE "TREATED"

- **I Am the LORD your God…. Worship No god but ME…**
- **Do not make for yourselves images of anything in heaven or on earth…**
- **Do not bow down to any idol or worship it, because I the LORD your God demand exclusive devotion, and I tolerate no rivals… [Got it – NO RIVALS]**
- **I bring punishment on those who hate ME (who don't believe in Him) and on their descendants… but, I show My love to thousands of generations to those who love Me and obey My Commandments."**

Very strangely, the Six Commandments that follow are the ONLY ones listed in the Books of Matthew, Mark, and Luke:

"Do not commit murder"

"Do not commit adultery"

"Do not accuse anybody falsely"

"Do not steal"

"Do not cheat"

"Respect your father and your mother"

It's impossible that these would have been the only Commandments mentioned by Jesus - none of them directly related to God as written in the New Testament, three times even?

Jesus, being a Prophet of God (not His son, since HE doesn't have one) could not have left out any of God's main Commandments

I say that 'simple' 'Common Sense' Is all it takes 'to know!'

CHAPTER 9

SAYINGS ATTRIBUTED TO JESUS IN THE NEW TESTAMENTTHAT HE COULDN'T HAVE SAID

W e've found that Jesus isn't the son of the One and Only Living God, as Jesus was said to be. God has nowhere in the Jewish Bible (Old Testament), or in the Qur'an said that HE has a son. Jesus, being a Prophet of God, as we've learned, couldn't say anything that God didn't tell him to say, as God had told Moses.

In His First Commandment, God firmly established that *'Only HE is God'* and that *'Only HE shall be worshipped'.* In the Gospels in the New Testament, a majority of texts were obviously modified, so as to sound as if Jesus had pronounced them.

Satan had undoubtedly inspired them by whispering his deceitful ideas into the minds of the new Christian Priesthood of the Roman Catholic Church to modify the writings left behind by the apostles of Jesus so as to fit the church's trinity religion established at Nicaea, where God's Prophet Jesus was made a god. Let's take a look at some of them.

John 14:5-6 The disciple Thomas asked Jesus after he was said to have told his disciples he was going to leave them and that he was going to prepare a place in heaven for them, which is totally questionable, "Lord, we do not know where you are going; so how do we know the way to get there?" Jesus has been quoted as saying, "*I am the way, the truth, and the life, no one goes to the Father except by me.*" Jesus could never have said this.

This is so, simply because he can't be (he isn't) the 'exclusive doorkeeper' to heaven, as those words declare.

Luke 17: (THE RAPTURE) Some Pharisees asked Jesus *when the Kingdom would come.* Among many other things Jesus has been attributed to have said: Luke 17:34-35, "On that night, I tell you, there will be two people sleeping in the same bed: one will be taken away, the other will be left behind. Two women will be grinding meal together: one will be taken away, the other will be left behind." (This has become known as 'the Rapture')

Someone with a very good imagination (Satan) induced this into the mind of somebody in the early Christian priesthood, who believed it and wrote it into the Bible, same as in the previous case). This is a situation that won't exist. But it allowed Messrs. Tim LaHaye and Jerry Jenkins to earn big money on their books 'Left Behind' and others that are related to this matter. I can only hope that some of the proceeds went to Charity.

God's teachings in the Qur'an that HE doesn't have a son are clear; therefore, Jesus, not being His son, isn't the god that Christianity determined Jesus to be.

When I read the introductory part of the Book of Revelation, I couldn't believe what John from Patmos is indicated to have said.

I'm totally sure that John's original writings didn't mention Jesus. This is so, because the dominant part of it is related to scores of end-of-time revelations that are unrelated to Jesus.

Adding in Jesus – which, by the way, I view as very clumsily done, mentioning him to be 'the lamb' - was for sure made after the formation of the Roman trinity Catholic Church, after the Nicaea Bishops Council in 325 AD.

The Introductory part – copied from the Internet - reads:

Revelation 1:1-3: "This book is the record of the events that Jesus Christ revealed. God (I can't even in my wildest fantasy imagine God having said any of this) gave him this revelation in order to show to his servants what must happen very soon. Christ made these things known to his servant John by sending his (?) angel to him, and John has told all that he had seen. This is his report concerning the message (that's said to be) from God and the truth revealed by Jesus Christ. Happy is the one who reads this book, and happy are those who listen to the words of this prophetic message and obey what is written, for the time is near when all these things will happen.

Revelation 1:8. *"I am the first and the last,"* says the Lord God Almighty, *"who is, who was, and who is to come".*

[What's said herein makes absolutely no sense, because why would God say of himself, *"and who is to come",* being that HE is the Eternal God, the one who is, who was, and will continue to exist forever?].

Revelation 1:9-10. Heading, *'A Vision of Christ'.* John speaks. "I am your brother, and as a follower of Jesus, I am your partner in patiently enduring the suffering that comes to those who belong to his Kingdom. I was put on the Island of Patmos because I had proclaimed God's word and the truth that Jesus revealed. On the Lord's Day, the Spirit took control of me, and I heard a loud voice that sounded like a trumpet, speaking behind me."

Revelation 1:12-18. "I (John) turned around to see who was talking to me, and I saw seven gold lamp-stands, and among them there was what looked like a human being, wearing a robe that reached to his feet, and a gold band around his chest. His hair was white as wool and his eyes blazed like fire; his feet shone like brass that has been refined and polished, and his voice sounded like a roaring waterfall. He held seven stars in his right hand, and a sharp two-edged sword came out of his mouth. His face was as bright as the midday sun. When I saw him, I fell down at his feet like a dead man."

He placed his right hand on me and said, *"Don't be afraid! I am the first and the last. I am the living one! I was dead, but now I am alive forever and ever. I have authority over death and the world of the dead."*

Having in mind what God revealed about Jesus in the Qur'an - described in chapter 4 above – we realize that what's said to have been written by John is a monstrous lie.

What's said can't have happened. I state that it's impossible that John could have obtained such a vision, describing the looks of who was supposed to be Jesus looking like God. But Jesus wasn't the *"First and the Last"*. Only God could say that of Himself, as HE says in Rev 1:8, not Jesus. Doubtless, there was a lot of rewriting, by people who didn't have the slightest idea of what they were doing, when they wrote.

Another statement, written in The Book of Revelation 22:13 attributed to Jesus that likewise is impossible he could have said, especially when his saying becomes compared to Rev 21:6, saying of *'The One (God) Who sits on the great white Throne'.*

Rev 22:12 "Listen!" says Jesus. "I am coming soon! I will bring my rewards with me, to give to each one according to what he (she) has done." – He goes on in Rev 22:13, as in Rev 1:8 above "*I am the first and the last, the beginning and the end.*"

This statement attributed to Jesus goes completely against what's written in Rev 21:6 copied below and Rev 1:8.

To get the essence, we need first to read Rev 20:11-16 where John writes, "Then I saw a great white throne and HE Who sits on it. Earth and heaven fled from His Presence and were seen no more and I saw the dead, great and small alike, standing in front of the throne. Books that included the Book of the Living were opened. The dead were judged according to what they had done during their lives on earth, as had been recorded by the 'guardian angel' in the respective 'Book of Deeds'. Then the sea gave up its dead. Death and the world of the dead also gave up the dead they held. And all were judged according to what they had done. Then death and the world of the dead were thrown into the lake of fire. (This lake of fire is the second death). Whoever did not have his (her) name written '*in the book of the living*' (because they had fallen away from the 'Right Way' of God) was thrown into the lake of fire."

(Now, let's check the following against Rev 22:13 above). Rev 21:5 John writes – "Then the One Who sits on the (great white) Throne (God) said." – "And now I (God) make all things new." – John goes on. HE (God) also said to me. "Write this, because these words are true and can be trusted." And HE (God) said, "*It is done! I Am the first and the last, the beginning and the end.*" – (Compare to what Jesus is attributed to have said in 22:13 above – exactly the same – Jesus could simply not have said it!).

CHAPTER 10

THE NEW ROMAN CHRISTIAN TRINITY CHURCH

The new Roman Christian trinity religion that resulted from the bishop's ecumenical conference in Nicaea has nothing in common with the Jewish monotheistic faith that God had given to His Prophet Moses, some fifteen hundred years earlier. Therefore, it's easy to see that the man-made (not from God) Christian trinity religion did not originate from God and isn't an 'Abrahamic religion', such as the Jewish and Islamic religions.

I felt compelled to add this chapter because of how Catholic paedophile (child molester) priests in Pennsylvania behaved against numerous defenceless little boys but also girls, ruining the lives of many of them. The sins committed by those priests and by so many other – including their superiors, bishops, archbishops and even Popes who protected the evildoers covering up what they had done – is like a 'scream of horror' that doubtless pleases Satan immensely.

We have learned how the man-made Christian Nicene Creed came to be, so we know that it wasn't God who originated it, but a bunch of unknowing bishops, who adopted the idea that

Jesus was the son of God from one man, Bishop Alexander from Alexandria, Egypt.

We need to understand that the priesthood in the new Roman Christian Catholic church were former pagans. Therefore, what they brought with them was obviously experiences from the rituals they performed to worship the idols of the respective cults to which they had belonged.

Now that was a major problem because God had told to Moses to stay away from all of that.

We need to understand the Laws of God are valid equally for every individual, whoever he or she is.

In the Book of Leviticus 18:30 God said, *"I am the Lord your God."* He ordered that the (Ten) Commandments HE gave *to Moses be obeyed (not only by the Jewish people, but by mankind.) HE also said that the practices and rituals of the people who lived in the land before* (pagans) were not to be followed. God also warned that the people would make itself unclean *by doing any of those things."*

In the Book of Deuteronomy 4:23-24, Moses told the people that they had to obey His Commandments *not to make for themselves any idol, because 'the LORD does not tolerate rivals'.*

In the Book of Deuteronomy 12:4, Moses told the people *not to worship God in the way that the* pagans *worship their gods.*

In Deuteronomy 12:30, Moses told the people to make *sure not to copy the religious practices of the pagans, **because that would be fatal.***

HE said many more things, that you can learn by reading this Book. But the new Christian priesthood not knowing any of what

God had told Moses not do, that would be fatal, went ahead and did exactly what the Jewish people had been told not to do.

Through His Prophet Isaiah 66:3-4 the LORD said that HE would bring disasters upon the people, because of their *disgusting ways of worship.*

Anybody who doesn't strictly follow His Laws, what HE Commanded is to be regarded a pagan and has no access to God. As HE said in Isaiah 66:4, t*hey chose to disobey Him and do evil.*

The misled bishops made Jesus into a god – and as such, a rival to the only living God. In His Commandments God very clearly said, "**HE *tolerates no rivals*.**" But Christians have been worshipping an inexistent rival to God instead of directing themselves to Him asking for His guidance with faith and belief.

Time has become very short to correct what has been wronged. It's up to each individual to get out of the snares of Satan.

CHAPTER 11

FOR THE RICH, TO ENTER GOD'S KINGDOM, IS AS DIFFICULT, as for a camel to get through the eye of a needle!

In this story, a rich man asked Jesus a question. He asked, "*Is there anything more I need to do?*"

Rich people pay careful attention to this, because Jesus didn't venture a joke. He was deadly serious and thinking of all of you when he answered the rich man, "*You need one more thing. Go, sell your possessions and give (the proceeds) to the poor, and you will have treasure in heaven. Then follow me.*"

When the rich man heard this, he went away sad, because he had great wealth.

Jesus said to his disciples, "*Truly I tell you it will be very hard for rich people to enter the Kingdom of heaven. It is much harder for a rich person to enter the kingdom of God than for a camel to go through a needle's eye.*"

When the disciples heard this, they were astonished and asked, "*Who then can be saved?*"

Jesus looked at them and said, *"For man it is impossible, but jointly with God everything is possible."*

My comment is that in today's world almost two-thousand years later, *'ruled as it is by Satan'* – it is practically impossible to enter the Kingdom of God – not just for the rich, but for mostly everybody. Don't believe this? Well, in the way that people are behaving with increasing wickedness, that's unfortunately the way it's going! Satan is doing the best he can to make it happen!

CHAPTER 12

THE PLACE OF THE LAW OF GOD

As we have learned, there exists only One Living God, the Creator of everything, who declared that – Only HE is God.

Given that there's only one God, it's obvious that only His Law and commandments is what counts for all of mankind. Therefore, the place of the LAW of God very obviously is 'up-front' and not hidden away as it has been.

When God's LAW isn't given the proper place in the Christian Bible, means committing a heinous sin that affects all Christians, but especially its priesthoods and very especially its leaders, and mainly the Popes.

Man-made creeds or laws, such as the Christian Nicene Creed aren't acceptable by God. The man-made rules instituted by the early Christian priesthood in the New Testament are insults against God since they doubtless were heavily re-written. The people who put it together will receive severe punishment. Please refer to what God said through the Prophet Isaiah 29:13-14 "These people claim to worship me, but what they say is worthless, and their hearts are someplace else. Their religion is nothing but man-made rules, which they have memorized. I will therefore startle them with unexpected blows. Those who are wise will turn out to be fools, and all their ingenuity will be worthless." God says it very clearly, 'religions governed by man-made rules, such as the Nicene Creed' aren't accepted by God. In other words, any and all religions, not having been put in place by God, aren't valid to God. In Isaiah 43:10 God declared that HE is the only God, there never was another (living) God and there never will be another God. Therefore, only His rules and His Laws are valid.

CHAPTER 13

THE CROSS OF CHRISTIANITY – AND ITS SYMBOLIZM

From what we learned in the foregoing, God made it clear in the Qur'an - that Jesus – His unique Prophet, not His son, and thus Not a god - was neither killed nor crucified. What HE reveals in the Qur'an 4:157 is that *"somebody else was made to resemble (look like) him (Jesus) to them (the Jews). They have no idea of what occurred because they were made to believe (by God) that he (Jesus) was crucified, so they believed it."* God goes on saying, *"But for certain, they did not crucify Jesus."*

The cross with a man (assumed to be Jesus), the symbol of Christianity - a trinity religion - isn't a religion of God, which we can easily make out from His commandments that HE had given to Moses, wherein HE established that only HE is God. In the Qur'an God also says "Don't say trinity". It's more than clear!

Putting in place the Christian trinity religion and everything it entails, replacing God's monotheistic religion added an immense victory to the many successes of Satan.

I view it as Satan's greatest Victory because it's interminably causing Christians to fall away from the way of God.

CHAPTER 14

THIS (LAST) CHAPTER CONTAINS WRITINGS THAT ARE MAINLY RELATED TO MATTERS OF THE END OF TIME.

14.1 MENTIONS ABOUT CHRISTIANITY BY NON-SCRIPTURE PROPHETS

This is copied from Chapter 5 in my book "*The Unfortunate destiny of our planet.*"

In this story about Jesus, there were two, who I call non-scripture Prophets, whose sayings are found in my book in Chapter 5. I'm providing (copying) the parts that are related to Christianity in the following, to complete the appalling picture of what's in the process of happening.

Prophecy of Merlin, wherein he said: "*The cult of religion shall be destroyed completely, and the ruins of the churches (Christian) shall be visible to everybody.*" (These are awesome revelations that Merlin and Tovazzo can only have obtained from the Only Living God) That tells us that Christianity is a false religion (Not of God).

Prophecies of unknown Italian 'Prophet' Gerolamo Tovazzo:

Tovazzo tells us that, *"Degenerate* (immoral, corrupt, perverted, decadent, etc.) *Rome will end in the ashes."* (This is an astounding Prophecy that goes 'Hand-in-hand' with what was revealed to John in the Book of Revelation 18:9.)

* *"When our time is at its end, Christians will* (realize that they) *for the most part are pagans".*

* *"The resurgence of faith will not come from rotten Rome, but from the East* (in all probability meaning 'Islam')."

* *"Their faith* (of the Christians), *will be on the money and in the power (to be in control); corruption and violence will triumph."*

14.2 THE APOSTLE JOHN - WHAT JESUS SAID ABOUT THE RULER

• John 12:31. "There will be a judging of this world and the ruler of this world (Satan) will be cast out."

• John 14:30. "I (Jesus) shall not speak much more with you (his Apostles) anymore, because *'the ruler of this world'* is coming."

• John 16:11. "... because the ruler of this world has been judged." (Satan was judged at the Creation of Adam when he disrespected God, Who cursed him and gave him respite until 'the Day of Recompense' or Judgment Day).

14.3 THE APOSTLE MARK – SAYINGS OF JESUS ABOUT THE END

• Mark 13:17-20. Jesus said, "How terrible it will be in those Days (at the End of Time). *For the trouble of those days (caused by Satan, the ruler of this world) will be far worse than any the* _world has ever known from the very beginning_ when God created the world (our Planet) until the present time." (Hitler's war and holocaust will seem small thing compared to what the evil Ruler is about to bring at the End.)

Mark 13:24. Jesus also said, something that God had told the Prophet Isaiah a long time before, "In the days after that time of trouble _the sun will grow dark, the moon will no longer shine,_ the stars will fall from heaven (it will look that at the tilting of Planet Earth). And the powers in space will be driven from their courses (Presumably the planets in our Solar System will lose their current orbits. See the pertaining prophecies of Merlin.)

• Mark 13:32. Jesus also said, _"No one knows when that day and hour_ (of the end) _will come, except God. "_

Today, it's possible to make a quite good approximation of when '_that time will come_', by comparing and studying all Prophecies and comparing them with current Scientific Reports of the effects of the Global Warming, how it's affecting the Oceans; and the situation in the world – that's becoming more and more volatile.

FINAL WORDS

Dear Reader,

*As you surely have observed, things on our planet aren't looking good
as we get closer to the end-of-time, as foretold by the All-mighty God.
Viewing how the 'global warming' or rather its effects are affecting our
planet, it's easy to realize that we are nearing the end.
I've written this book, to provide guidance to mainly Christians,
so, you learn why you need to change your beliefs.
What has been difficult to deal with, are the many texts that are corrupted,
putting in place situations in the scriptures that are false.
Those scriptures were used inadvertent of their falseness. Worst of all, it led
to the taking away of many people (including most Christians) from God,
as Satan told God he would do, as God reveals in the Qur'an.
It's my hope that you will take advantage of and use
the knowledge contained in this book to do the required changes.
It's in your best interest to do it because those who don't,
will be making company with Satan in Hell for all eternity!*

Index

THE END